JUAN PERÓN

JUAN PERÓN

John DeChancie

CHELSEA HOUSE PUBLISHERS

NEW YORK

NEW HAVEN   PHILADELPHIA

EDITOR-IN-CHIEF: Nancy Toff
EXECUTIVE EDITOR: Remmel T. Nunn
MANAGING EDITOR: Karyn Gullen Browne
COPY CHIEF: Perry Scott King
ART DIRECTOR: Giannella Garrett
PICTURE EDITOR: Elizabeth Terhune

Staff for JUAN PERÓN:

SENIOR EDITOR: John W. Selfridge
ASSISTANT EDITORS: Maria Behan, Pierre Hauser, Kathleen McDermott, Bert Yaeger
COPY EDITORS: Gillian Bucky, Sean Dolan
DESIGN ASSISTANT: Jill Goldreyer
PICTURE RESEARCH: Matthew Miller
LAYOUT: David Murray
PRODUCTION COORDINATOR: Alma Rodriguez
COVER ILLUSTRATION: Kye Carbone

CREATIVE DIRECTOR: Harold Steinberg

Frontispiece courtesy of UPI/Bettmann Newsphotos

   3   5   7   9   8   6   4   2

Library of Congress Cataloging in Publication Data

DeChancie, John. JUAN PERÓN

(World leaders past & present)
Bibliography: p.
Includes index.
1. Perón, Juan Domingo, 1895–1974—Juvenile literature.
2. Argentina—Politics and government—1943–1955—
Juvenile literature. 3. Argentina—Politics and government—
1955–1983—Juvenile literature. 4. Argentina—Presidents—
Biography—Juvenile literature. [1. Perón, Juan Domingo,
1895–1974. 2. Heads of state. 3. Argentina—History—
1943–   .] I. Title. II. Series.
F2849.P48D43   1987   982'.062'0924 [B] [92]
86-31749

ISBN 0-87754-548-0

Contents

CHELSEA HOUSE PUBLISHERS

WORLD LEADERS PAST & PRESENT

ON LEADERSHIP
Arthur M. Schlesinger, jr.

LEADERSHIP, it may be said, is really what makes the world go round. Love no doubt smooths the passage; but love is a private transaction between consenting adults. Leadership is a public transaction with history. The idea of leadership affirms the capacity of individuals to move, inspire, and mobilize masses of people so that they act together in pursuit of an end. Sometimes leadership serves good purposes, sometimes bad; but whether the end is benign or evil, great leaders are those men and women who leave their personal stamp on history.

Now, the very concept of leadership implies the proposition that individuals can make a difference. This proposition has never been universally accepted. From classical times to the present day, eminent thinkers have regarded individuals as no more than the agents and pawns of larger forces, whether the gods and goddesses of the ancient world or, in the modern era, race, class, nation, the dialectic, the will of the people, the spirit of the times, history itself. Against such forces, the individual dwindles into insignificance.

So contends the thesis of historical determinism. Tolstoy's great novel *War and Peace* offers a famous statement of the case. Why, Tolstoy asked, did millions of men in the Napoleonic wars, denying their human feelings and their common sense, move back and forth across Europe slaughtering their fellows? "The war," Tolstoy answered, "was bound to happen simply because it was bound to happen." All prior history predetermined it. As for leaders, they, Tolstoy said, "are but the labels that serve to give a name to an end and, like labels, they have the least possible connection with the event." The greater the leader, "the more conspicuous the inevitability and the predestination of every act he commits." The leader, said Tolstoy, is "the slave of history."

Determinism takes many forms. Marxism is the determinism of class. Nazism the determinism of race. But the idea of men and women as the slaves of history runs athwart the deepest human instincts. Rigid determinism abolishes the idea of human freedom—

the assumption of free choice that underlies every move we make, every word we speak, every thought we think. It abolishes the idea of human responsibility, since it is manifestly unfair to reward or punish people for actions that are by definition beyond their control. No one can live consistently by any deterministic creed. The Marxist states prove this themselves by their extreme susceptibility to the cult of leadership.

More than that, history refutes the idea that individuals make no difference. In December 1931 a British politician crossing Park Avenue in New York City between 76th and 77th Streets around 10:30 P.M. looked in the wrong direction and was knocked down by an automobile—a moment, he later recalled, of a man aghast, a world aglare: "I do not understand why I was not broken like an eggshell or squashed like a gooseberry." Fourteen months later an American politician, sitting in an open car in Miami, Florida, was fired on by an assassin; the man beside him was hit. Those who believe that individuals make no difference to history might well ponder whether the next two decades would have been the same had Mario Constasino's car killed Winston Churchill in 1931 and Giuseppe Zangara's bullet killed Franklin Roosevelt in 1933. Suppose, in addition, that Adolf Hitler had been killed in the street fighting during the Munich *Putsch* of 1923 and that Lenin had died of typhus during World War I. What would the 20th century be like now?

For better or for worse, individuals do make a difference. "The notion that a people can run itself and its affairs anonymously," wrote the philosopher William James, "is now well known to be the silliest of absurdities. Mankind does nothing save through initiatives on the part of inventors, great or small, and imitation by the rest of us—these are the sole factors in human progress. Individuals of genius show the way, and set the patterns, which common people then adopt and follow."

Leadership, James suggests, means leadership in thought as well as in action. In the long run, leaders in thought may well make the greater difference to the world. But, as Woodrow Wilson once said, "Those only are leaders of men, in the general eye, who lead in action. . . . It is at their hands that new thought gets its translation into the crude language of deeds." Leaders in thought often invent in solitude and obscurity, leaving to later generations the tasks of imitation. Leaders in action—the leaders portrayed in this series—have to be effective in their own time.

And they cannot be effective by themselves. They must act in response to the rhythms of their age. Their genius must be adapted, in a phrase of William James's, "to the receptivities of the moment." Leaders are useless without followers. "There goes the mob," said the French politician hearing a clamor in the streets. "I am their leader. I must follow them." Great leaders turn the inchoate emotions of the mob to purposes of their own. They seize on the opportunities of their time, the hopes, fears, frustrations, crises, potentialities. They succeed when events have prepared the way for them, when the community is awaiting to be aroused, when they can provide the clarifying and organizing ideas. Leadership ignites the circuit between the individual and the mass and thereby alters history.

It may alter history for better or for worse. Leaders have been responsible for the most extravagant follies and most monstrous crimes that have beset suffering humanity. They have also been vital in such gains as humanity has made in individual freedom, religious and racial tolerance, social justice and respect for human rights.

There is no sure way to tell in advance who is going to lead for good and who for evil. But a glance at the gallery of men and women in *World Leaders—Past and Present* suggests some useful tests.

One test is this: do leaders lead by force or by persuasion? By command or by consent? Through most of history leadership was exercised by the divine right of authority. The duty of followers was to defer and to obey. "Theirs not to reason why,/ Theirs but to do and die." On occasion, as with the so-called "enlightened despots" of the 18th century in Europe, absolutist leadership was animated by humane purposes. More often, absolutism nourished the passion for domination, land, gold and conquest and resulted in tyranny.

The great revolution of modern times has been the revolution of equality. The idea that all people should be equal in their legal condition has undermined the old structure of authority, hierarchy and deference. The revolution of equality has had two contrary effects on the nature of leadership. For equality, as Alexis de Tocqueville pointed out in his great study *Democracy in America*, might mean equality in servitude as well as equality in freedom.

"I know of only two methods of establishing equality in the political world," Tocqueville wrote. "Rights must be given to every citizen, or none at all to anyone . . . save one, who is the master of all." There was no middle ground "between the sovereignty of all and the absolute power of one man." In his astonishing prediction of 20th-century totalitarian dictatorship, Tocqueville explained how the revolution of equality could lead to the *"Führerprinzip"* and more terrible absolutism than the world had ever known.

But when rights are given to every citizen and the sovereignty of all is established, the problem of leadership takes a new form, becomes more exacting than ever before. It is easy to issue commands and enforce them by the rope and the stake, the concentration camp and the *gulag*. It is much harder to use argument and achievement to overcome opposition and win consent. The Founding Fathers of the United States understood the difficulty. They believed that history had given them the opportunity to decide, as Alexander Hamilton wrote in the first Federalist Paper, whether men are indeed capable of basing government on "reflection and choice, or whether they are forever destined to depend . . . on accident and force."

Government by reflection and choice called for a new style of leadership and a new quality of followership. It required leaders to be responsive to popular concerns, and it required followers to be active and informed participants in the process. Democracy does not eliminate emotion from politics; sometimes it fosters demagoguery; but it is confident that, as the greatest of democratic leaders put it, you cannot fool all of the people all of the time. It measures leadership by results and retires those who overreach or falter or fail.

It is true that in the long run despots are measured by results too. But they can postpone the day of judgment, sometimes indefinitely, and in the meantime they can do infinite harm. It is also true that democracy is no guarantee of virtue and intelligence in government, for the voice of the people is not necessarily the voice of God. But democracy, by assuring the right of opposition, offers built-in resistance to the evils inherent in absolutism. As the theologian Reinhold Niebuhr summed it up, "Man's capacity for justice makes democracy possible, but man's inclination to injustice makes democracy necessary."

A second test for leadership is the end for which power is sought. When leaders have as their goal the supremacy of a master race or the promotion of totalitarian revolution or the acquisition and exploitation of colonies or the protection of greed and privilege or the preservation of personal power, it is likely that their leadership will do little to advance the cause of humanity. When their goal is the abolition of slavery, the liberation of women, the enlargement of opportunity for the poor and powerless, the extension of equal rights to racial minorities, the defense of the freedoms of expression and opposition, it is likely that their leadership will increase the sum of human liberty and welfare.

Leaders have done great harm to the world. They have also conferred great benefits. You will find both sorts in this series. Even "good" leaders must be regarded with a certain wariness. Leaders are not demigods; they put on their trousers one leg after another just like ordinary mortals. No leader is infallible, and every leader needs to be reminded of this at regular intervals. Irreverence irritates leaders but is their salvation. Unquestioning submission corrupts leaders and demands followers. Making a cult of a leader is always a mistake. Fortunately hero worship generates its own antidote. "Every hero," said Emerson, "becomes a bore at last."

The signal benefit the great leaders confer is to embolden the rest of us to live according to our own best selves, to be active, insistent, and resolute in affirming our own sense of things. For great leaders attest to the reality of human freedom against the supposed inevitabilities of history. And they attest to the wisdom and power that may lie within the most unlikely of us, which is why Abraham Lincoln remains the supreme example of great leadership. A great leader, said Emerson, exhibits new possibilities to all humanity. "We feed on genius. . . . Great men exist that there may be greater men."

Great leaders, in short, justify themselves by emancipating and empowering their followers. So humanity struggles to master its destiny, remembering with Alexis de Tocqueville: "It is true that around every man a fatal circle is traced beyond which he cannot pass; but within the wide verge of that circle he is powerful and free; as it is with man, so with communities."

1

The Seventeenth of October

The Plaza de Mayo had been filling up with workers during the course of the day, and by nightfall
the crowd had swelled to nearly a quarter-million.
It was mid-October, the start of summer in the
Southern Hemisphere, and the day was hot. Many
of the men in the crowd had taken off their shirts,
and all day long people had been wading and bath-
ing in the plaza's many fountains. Now darkness
came, and people rolled newspapers into torches
and lit them. All eyes turned toward the end of the
plaza and the pink stone government building
known as the *Casa Rosada*, "the Pink House." The
crowd waited for an appearance of the man they had
come to cheer, the man whose name they had been
chanting all day.

The place was Argentina, the year 1945, and the
man of the hour was Juan Domingo Perón, who
until very recently had been the vice-president of
the country. His supporters, the industrial workers
of Argentina, wanted him to take the reins of power
from a presidency crippled by scandal and political
conflict. He was their champion. Perón knew it, and
this was his hour of triumph. What made the taste
of victory even sweeter was the fact that this sudden
rise to power followed hard on the heels of his resignation from office and arrest by the army officers
he once commanded.

> *I always work best in the
> midst of an uproar.*
> —JUAN PERÓN

**Juan Domingo Perón, the charismatic and controversial
president of Argentina from 1946 to 1955 and 1973 to
1974. A recent biographer evaluates the impact of Perón's successes and failures by saying: "For Argentines,
understanding Perón is prerequisite to understanding
themselves."**

October 1945, Buenos Aires: Nearly a quarter-million of Perón's supporters gathered to demand the former vice-president's return to power. It was Argentina's first workers' rally for political change.

For the past five days, Buenos Aires had buzzed with rumors. It was known that Colonel Perón had been arrested, but his whereabouts had been kept secret by the government. President Edelmiro Farrell had ordered an arrest without specifying charges, partly to prevent Perón from organizing an uprising by his supporters in labor and partly to protect Perón from his enemies. Even an unsuccessful assassination attempt could trigger violent demonstrations. At this moment, as the crowds chanted in the Plaza de Mayo, Perón was in a military hospital in Buenos Aires, having been released from prison the day before. A friend and a supporter of his, Dr. Mazza, had used a lung X ray to convince the president that the humidity of Perón's island prison was endangering the colonel's health. He was safe and well, but his short exile had tested his strength of character.

Perón was milking the dramatic situation for all it was worth, waiting for the crowds in the Plaza de Mayo to reach maximum size. Then, and only then, would he act. His many supporters — labor leaders, sympathetic politicians, and military officers — flitted about his hospital suite, plotting, scheming, and offering advice.

"We must seize the moment," one of Perón's right-hand men told him.

Perón merely nodded calmly and lit a cigarette. He strolled about the suite in his red smoking jacket, smiling, confident, in control. He was a big, thickly built man, with dark hair swept back from a high forehead. His nose was prominent and his eyes looked small in his wide face. There was a determined, defiant curl to the line of his mouth. In this unfolding political drama he looked very much the part of the main character, the protagonist, the man of action; and when he spoke he did so forcefully, plainly, sometimes even bluntly.

"Perónistas" like these demonstrators considered Perón a champion of the common man. Many were industrial workers, long neglected and exploited by Argentina's previous governments.

Rich in natural resources, the South American nation of Argentina is the world's eighth largest country and has a great variety of terrains. The Argentine people are predominantly of Spanish and western-European descent.

But appearances can be deceiving. There was more to the man than was indicated by his often brash, crude exterior, and there was a woman nearby who knew it. She was Eva Duarte, a popular radio and stage actress, and she had been Perón's companion and confidante for almost two years. Evita, as she was known, had spent the last few days trying to marshal support for Perón. The extent and effectiveness of her efforts to rescue her friend from prison is open to debate, but there is no question of her importance in the legendary career of Juan Domingo Perón. In fact, Evita was destined to become somewhat of a legend herself.

Perón put out his cigarette. It was time to begin the series of behind-the-scenes maneuvers that would return him to power.

For the crowds of workers standing vigil in front of the Casa Rosada, the evening wore on. The plaza was sweltering. Palm trees hung limply in the humid, unmoving air.

Then, finally, at a little after 11 P.M., Perón stepped out on a balcony of the Casa Rosada. The crowd went wild. Their hero was safe and sound and apparently a free man. They cheered, they shouted, they screamed until they were hoarse, tears streaming from their eyes. Paper torches heated the already torrid night. The demonstration continued for 15 minutes.

Gauchos in typical riding clothes. The gauchos, whose horsemanship was legendary, played a historical role similar to that of American cowboys in settling the grassy ranchlands of the Argentine north.

Finally, Perón spoke. Deeply moved, he first asked the assembled workers to sing the national anthem. This they did, and afterward he told his supporters that this day was the greatest in Argentina's political history and that this mass demonstration of support was a great "celebration of democracy." It was an important day for Argentine labor, marking the first time that workers had rallied to force changes in the government. Perón told the workers that he felt close to all of them. Caught up in the emotion of the moment, he said, "I want to hug this huge mass of humanity and press it close to my heart as I would my own mother."

Young Perón (left) with his brother and mother. His early years on small, isolated ranches taught him to endure hardship and enjoy the outdoors and athletics.

The crowd interrupted him frequently with shouted questions. "Where were you?" they wanted to know. "Who put you in prison? Who was responsible?" But Perón would not hear of laying blame. This was a time for unity, he said, for forgiveness. Fraternal love was the order of the day. He then urged the workers to return home peacefully and spend the next day celebrating their victory. The crowd immediately took up the chant:

Tomorrow's the feast of Saint Perón
The bosses will be on their own!

It was to become the slogan of the Peronist movement.

There was more cheering; more pledges of love and fraternity were made. Perón embraced his friends on the balcony, then turned again to the teeming multitude of workers, clasping his hands over his head like a boxer, basking in the glory of the moment. The torches waved, the cheering went on, and on, and on.

At last, Perón left the balcony, and the seventeenth of October ended. Argentina would never be the same again.

Arrest and exile, return and triumph, all in less than a week. This abrupt reversal of fortunes represented one of the most amazing turnabouts in political history. To understand how it could happen, it is necessary to explore the cultural and historical background of Argentine politics.

Argentina's name comes from the Latin word for silver, *argentum*. To the Spanish explorers of the 16th century, the Atlantic coast of the southern tip of South America was the Silver Land. The Spaniards hoped to find mountains of silver there. They didn't, but they found something worth more.

Argentina is a country of great scenic beauty, rich natural resources, many different climates, and passionate, freedom-loving people. In the north, its dominant geographical feature is the *pampa*, the vast grassy plain across which roam numerous herds of cattle. Where cattle do not graze, wheat grows. Argentina is one of the world's great beef and grain producers. Most of the pampa is divided into

> [The gaucho] was above all things a horseman, never dismounting from his animal except to sleep beside it. . . . Round him clings all the romance of the Pampas, for he was taken as the embodiment of the primitive virtues of daring, endurance, and loyalty.
> —JAMES BRYCE
> American writer

A prosperous street in Buenos Aires as it appeared in 1924. Perón faced a difficult adjustment at the age of nine; he left his family to study in Buenos Aires.

large privately owned ranches called *estancias*. But not all of the country is fertile plain. The southern third of Argentina, a region called Patagonia, lies not far from the Antarctic Circle. Patagonia is cold, rugged, and barren, but hardly worthless; it contains substantial oil reserves and is rich in iron, tin, zinc, and aluminum ore. Millions of sheep graze on its sturdy grasses.

The snow-capped Andes form Argentina's long western border with Chile. The west is dry, almost desert. Cacti are plentiful, and much of the terrain looks like the southwestern United States.

Argentina is ethnically diverse, but the mixture is mostly western European. The majority of the population is of Spanish ancestry, but there are also people of Italian, British, German, Dutch, and French descent. Indians and mestizos (a Spanish-Indian mixture) make up less than three percent of the population.

The ruggedness of the country — the free-spirited, untamed wildness of it — is personified in the figure of the *gaucho*, the Argentine cowboy. In his red poncho, spurred boots, and voluminous riding pants, atop a horse, he cuts a romantic figure riding across much of the country's tumultuous early history.

And in modern times we find another figure shrouded in a fascinating, romantic mystique, a man who would carry the image of the gaucho into the 20th century, first as a distinguished army officer and then as a charismatic leader of his people.

Juan Domingo Perón was born on October 8, 1895, in the village of Lobos, which lies about 56 miles southwest of Buenos Aires. Like most Argentines, he was of mixed European ancestry and probably had some Indian forebears as well. His father, Mario Tomás Perón, was a tenant farmer who married a servant girl by the name of Juana Toledo. She bore him two sons, the second of whom was Juan Domingo. Young Juan's memories of the village of Lobos were destined to grow dim, for in 1899 his father wearied of farm life and moved the family to a sheep ranch in remote Patagonia. The region, then as now, was sparsely populated. There were many more sheep than people.

Life on the estancia was sometimes harsh, especially during winter. The first Perón homestead — not nearly as big as the typical huge estancia of the region — was near Río Gallegos, which lies near the southern tip of South America. The climate there is sometimes antarctic. One particularly trying winter forced the family to relocate to northern Pata-

Perón was a champion fencer, horseman, and athlete while a military cadet. At 15 he abandoned plans to study medicine in favor of a military career.

A view of the National Military College athletic field. Perón's military career progressed steadily after he graduated from the college and was commissioned into the infantry; his strong leadership skills first emerged after he became a military teacher in 1920.

gonia, where they settled on another ranch. (In the Southern Hemisphere, warmer climates generally lie to the north, toward the equator.)

Growing up in this rugged country, Juan Domingo learned to love the outdoors and to enjoy athletics. He became an accomplished horseman at an early age. Formal education, however, was not easily available, and at the age of nine Juan left the ranch to go to school in Buenos Aires, staying with relatives during the school year and going back home only during summer vacations.

It was a difficult adjustment for him, but he later maintained that being thrust out on his own at a tender age taught him self-reliance. He was a fair student, and as he progressed to higher grades he began to prepare for medical school. At some point, however, he changed his choice of career. Perhaps at the urging of friends, or perhaps on a whim, Juan bypassed the medical school entrance examination and took the one for the army military academy. He passed the test and was admitted to the National Military College. He was not yet 16 years old.

Life as a cadet suited young Perón. The rigors of military training were nothing compared to the hardships he had endured in Patagonia. His academic grades were average — though he excelled in horsemanship, fencing, and other athletic activities — but he did well enough to graduate and receive his commission. On December 13, 1913, he entered the infantry as a second lieutenant.

Perón's early military career was quiet, routine, and perhaps a trifle dull, as is usually the case in a peacetime army. He served in an infantry regiment at various locations and was promoted to first lieutenant in 1915. His career progressed steadily, if not brilliantly, and in 1920 he became an instructor in a noncommissioned officers' school near Buenos Aires. It was here that Perón first showed evidence of outstanding leadership skills. He became an excellent instructor who inspired admiration and loyalty in the men he commanded. His personal appeal was considerable, and he began to gather about him a group of loyal followers who would stay with him throughout his life and career.

Promotions came. He attained the rank of captain in 1924, and in 1926 he began attending the army's college for advanced military studies, where he spent the next three years. It was during this period that he met, courted, and married his first wife, Aurelia Tizón, the daughter of a local commercial photographer. Perón was more than a dozen years her senior, but this was not unusual by Argentine conventions. They were married early in 1929. It was not the happiest of occasions because shortly before the wedding Perón's father died.

From 1930 to 1936 Perón was a professor of military history at the war college, at the same time serving as a private secretary to the minister of war and as an aide to senior officers. It was a period of internal dissension in Argentina's government, and Perón found himself in the midst of it.

2

Professor Perón

The constitutionally established government of Argentina, only 77 years old by 1930, had never been a smoothly running operation. After the War of Independence from Spain was successfully concluded in 1819, the country found itself in a state of virtual anarchy. The most important of the estancia owners feuded among themselves to become local *caudillos* (quasi-feudal overlords with armies of gauchos), and caudillos fought with the more cosmopolitan, outward-looking *porteños* (port-city dwellers) for control of the country. The country more or less united under a caudillo named Juan Manuel de Rosas in 1835, but it was opposition to his rule of terror that finally united the major caudillos and the Buenos Aires liberals in 1852. They forced Rosas into exile and in 1853 drew up a constitution, modeled primarily on the United States Constitution. This document provided for democratically elected legislatures at provincial and federal levels and also created the office of president. All government officials, including the president, were to be chosen by free elections.

> *Every Argentine has political opinions as well as an unswerving conviction of their soundness. The result is a refusal to compromise, along with a tendency to extremism in both rhetoric and behavior.*
> —JOSEPH A. PAGE
> Perón biographer

The political climate of Perón's youth and early adulthood was ambiguous. Despite a constitution that promised democracy, the elite conservative landowners continued to dominate the economy.

Argentina's first two presidents governed a nation divided by regional conflicts. Not until 1862 did Bartolomé Mitre, possibly the greatest of the Argentine presidents, establish a unified republic. After Mitre's term ended in 1868 the constitutional system continued to work to a degree, but control of the government was firmly in the hands of the conservative landed elite, the owners of the great estancias, who largely dominated the economy. They effectively denied the growing urban middle class political representation until 1889, when a new party called the Radical Civic Union was formed. The Radicals (who were actually fairly conservative; they soon gained the support of much of the aristocracy) advocated free-enterprise economics, electoral reform, and expanded suffrage. The party won power in 1916 when the Radical candidate, Hipólito Irigoyen, was elected president. He served a six-year term, waited out the next term, then was elected

Argentine troops on maneuvers in 1926. The military exerted significant political power and grew increasingly suspicious of the effectiveness of civilian rule at the close of the 1920s.

president again in 1928. (The constitution did not permit immediate reelection.) When he took office the second time he was 76 years old, and by 1930 there was talk that the old man was verging on senility. The Radical party itself had come under increasing fire from its constituents — the aristocracy and the urban working class — since coming to power in 1916. Irigoyen did nothing to strengthen the economic position of the middle class. Rather, he perpetuated the aristocracy-based economy by continuing to export large quantities of grain and meat and import manufactured goods instead of encouraging the growth of local industry. These and other problems, such as charges of corruption, had eroded Radical power to the extent that two different factions of army officers were considering a coup d'état. Many opposed Irigoyen's autocratic methods and the personality cult he fostered.

By the early years of the century, the Argentine military had grown into a considerable political force. It had ties to the conservative landed elite, and it tended to be deeply suspicious of, and sometimes hostile to, civilian rule. Irigoyen's civilian leadership especially upset them, given his political favoritism and use of the army in provincial interventions for political gain. Influenced by the rise of the Fascists in Italy and the growing power of the National Socialist German Workers' party (Nazis) in Germany in the 1920s, one group of officers, led by General José F. Uriburu, saw authoritarianism as the only efficient way to govern a country. Another group of military officers, led by General Agustín P. Justo, wanted to keep the civilian government and strengthen the constitution. The conspiracy group was led by antidemocratic generals, who sought the abolition of all political parties and the establishment of a military government that excluded civilian participation.

The Uriburu ringleaders persuaded Perón to join them in June 1930, and he worked for their cause through the summer. When it appeared that the plot would not succeed, Perón withdrew his support and joined the group led by Justo. This did not stop the conspirators, for on September 6, 1930, army

THE BETTMANN ARCHIVE

Bartolomé Mitre, the first president to govern a unified Argentina. After Mitre's term ended in 1868 the constitutional system worked only to a limited degree, mainly for the benefit of the great *estancia* owners.

Only a miracle would save the revolution. The people of Buenos Aires, who in a human avalanche spilled into the streets shouting 'Long live the revolution,' made this miracle.
—JUAN PERÓN
on the revolution of 1930

People take to the streets of Buenos Aires on September 6, 1930, after learning an army faction has overthrown their civilian government. Perón's change of allegiance shortly before the coup cost him the favor of the new Argentine leaders.

troops marched on the capital. Perón himself was in the thick of the commotion in the streets, doing his best to limit the loss of life and possible damage to government property.

The coup was successful, and the Argentine Supreme Court gave legal recognition to the new military government. Because Perón had switched sides, he was out of favor, and as a result lost his government post as an aide to the minister of war. Uriburu's policies brought so much resistance that he was forced to call for elections in November 1931. General Justo and his coalition party — composed mainly of Conservatives, with some Radical and Socialist support — were voted in (albeit with a lot of vote tampering). Perón soon regained his assignment and was promoted to major in December 1931. He continued to teach at the war college, at the same time embarking on a career as an author. He published several volumes of military history.

In his capacity as professor, Perón continued to improve his public-speaking skills, giving lectures both at the college and in the government itself. One lecture dealt with neighboring Chile and its possible expansionist designs on Patagonia. Perhaps because Perón was seen as somewhat of an expert on Chile, he was sent to Santiago, the capital of that country, as a military attaché (technical expert) to the Argentine embassy.

This episode in Perón's life is shrouded in controversy. It is clear that Perón, doubtless acting under orders, was involved in attempts to gather intelligence in Chile by whatever means were necessary, which amounted to spying. It is not clear whether the Chilean government expelled him for this activity. Perón never denied that he had been a spy but always denied the charge that he had been caught in the act. Perhaps he left Chile just in time. An Argentine spy ring was exposed shortly after his departure. At any rate, the affair did not adversely affect his military career, but it marked the first time Perón played a major part in a controversy. It would not be the last.

More dark clouds appeared. In 1938 Perón's wife died of cancer. They had no children.

After a few months' personal leave, he was back in Buenos Aires, looking for something to keep him occupied. Later in 1939 an opportunity arose. He was assigned to an Italian army division training for mountain warfare in the Alps. Italian and German military training courses were traditional in orientation and were very highly regarded. Years later Perón would claim that his orders again included the gathering of intelligence, this time concerning the impending war in Europe.

The trip was a welcome antidote to the emptiness and restlessness he felt. In February 1939 Juan Perón left Argentina on a passenger liner bound for Italy, where he would live for two years.

The experience was to impress him greatly.

General José F. Uriburu (center, in uniform), leader of the 1930 coup, was in power for only one year. Weathering the coup, Perón continued to teach and to write about military history.

3

War and Revolution

In 1939 the pall of impending war hung over Europe. Nazi Germany, having annexed Austria, parts of Czechoslovakia, and other territory, was now threatening the Polish border and making plans to invade that country. France and Great Britain had pledged to protect Polish security. There was to be no turning back from a collision course. A second world war seemed inevitable.

Italy, under its Fascist dictator Benito Mussolini, had allied with Germany and Japan to form the Axis powers. Argentina, staunchly noninterventionist as a result of its experience with British invasion attempts in 1806 and 1807, declared itself neutral. The Argentine military establishment did not consider its continued association with Italy and Germany as Axis alignment. Perón and his men were guests of the Italian army, and at first the stay may have seemed like a vacation. The mountain warfare course included skiing instruction. Photographs taken at the time show a smiling Perón on skis enjoying himself. However, on September 1 the opening guns of World War II put an end to the holiday. Perón served with alpine army units until the end of May 1940. The units Perón served with were not actively involved in the fighting. For the next seven months Perón assisted the military attaché at the Argentine embassy in Rome. He managed to see

> *Perón saw nothing morally repugnant about Nazi Germany or Fascist Italy. He viewed them through the prism of his military background and found many features of both systems of government admirable. The fact that trains ran on time counted for a great deal, while the absence of free speech did not disturb him.*
> —JOSEPH A. PAGE
> Perón biographer

The totalitarian dictatorships in Italy and Germany were observed firsthand by Perón during the early years of World War II. Many of their methods greatly impressed and influenced him.

some of the rest of Europe before going back to Buenos Aires. In the spring of 1940 Perón visited German-occupied France and also went to Berlin, Budapest, and parts of Albania. He traveled through Spain as well and saw the devastation left behind by its civil war.

But what impressed Perón most were his first-hand observations of the internal workings of Fascist Italy. What he saw there affected the future development of his political thinking.

Fascism, as devised by Benito Mussolini, is a type of government in which one party, headed by a strong ruler, has sole power. Political opposition is put down by force, and industry, under tight governmental control, is kept in the hands of private owners. A belligerent nationalism dominates the outlook on the rest of the world. Later, Germany's Adolf Hitler adopted this political philosophy and added fanatical anti-Semitism to form the basis of Nazi ideology. The charge of fascism has often been made against Perón, and there is no denying that he felt nothing but admiration for Mussolini's Italy. He saw it as an extremely well run country with a good sense of organization and discipline, attri-

Mussolini addressing a vast crowd in 1938. Perón was particularly impressed by Mussolini's use of mass political spectacles to promote public support. In later years Perón used similar mass rallies in building his own political career.

Benito Mussolini, leader of
the Italian Fascists. Perón
admired the compelling ef-
ficiency of the Fascist system, but he could not foresee
the ultimate defeat and humiliation Italy would suffer
as its result.

butes that must have appealed to his soldier's way
of thinking. The trains ran on time, and the country
seemed to have a sense of direction and purpose.
That this direction ultimately would lead to Italy's
defeat and humiliation was not apparent in the days
when German boots were heard goose-stepping all
over Europe. Victory for the Axis powers seemed
assured in 1940. France was beaten, Great Britain
was alone, the United States was officially neutral,
and the Soviet Union had signed a nonaggression
pact with Germany in August 1939. But the course
of events was to change drastically, and when it did,
so too did Perón's views.

Nevertheless, in 1940 he admired Mussolini as a
leader and was particularly impressed with his
use of mass political spectacles. The crowds, the

speeches, the parades, the ranks of marching Black-shirts (Fascist party members wore black uniforms) were especially effective in promoting public support. Much of what Perón saw and experienced would be put to good use in his own political career.

The charge that Perón admired fascism must be given some credence; however, this is not to say that he was committed to fascism or that he envisioned this sort of political system for Argentina. Labels tend to be misleading at best, and political realities are often at odds with ideology. Perón had his own ideas about how his country should be run.

Perón later wrote that he was much taken with the way in which Italy's Fascists controlled the nation's trade unions. What Perón learned and observed about unions and the techniques of mass mobilization of workers for political ends would figure greatly in the evolution of his political thinking.

Adolf Hitler, the German Nazi dictator, borrowed many elements of Mussolini's Fascist system. He suppressed all political opposition and imposed strict government controls on production. His policy of extreme anti-Semitism led to the deaths of 6 million Jews.

Perón returned to Argentina in December 1940 and was assigned to teach mountain warfare to troops stationed in Mendoza, a western town high in the Andes. He stayed there for over a year, then returned to the Campo de Mayo, the army headquarters in Buenos Aires. By this time he was a full colonel. Settling down to a high administrative position, he found the army command divided over the issue of Argentina's relations with the Axis powers. The United States had declared war on Japan after the bombing of Pearl Harbor in December 1941. At a hastily assembled conference of Western Hemisphere powers in January 1942, the United States had all but demanded that Central and South American governments cut diplomatic relations with Axis powers and help secure the Western Hemisphere from outside attack. Argentina and Chile resisted the call, agreeing only to consider a recommendation that they break diplomatic ties. Out of unabashed sympathy for fascism and nazism, some officers wanted to maintain diplomatic relations with the Axis powers. Others favored the Allies

A pro-Axis youth rally in Buenos Aires in 1942. During World War II widespread identification with extreme nationalistic philosophies challenged Argentina's traditional ties with the countries of the Allied front.

The firing of General Pedro Ramírez precipitated a crisis in 1943. Pro-Axis officers of the Group of United Officers (GOU) overthrew the Conservative government; two days later, Ramírez himself was named president.

(Great Britain, the United States, the Soviet Union, and their allies) and also wanted a new government that was not dominated by the Conservatives, who had been in power since the coup of 1930. A third group wanted to preserve Argentina's neutrality. Argentina maintained diplomatic relations with the Axis powers until 1944, breaking these ties only in the face of intense economic pressure from the United States.

Perón knew where his sympathies lay. A secret club known as the Group of United Officers (GOU) formed within the army, and Perón soon became its leading member. The members of the GOU were generally right wing and pro-Axis, but they argued for a variety of themes and goals in order to attract a greater number of supporters. In the end the GOU seemed to unite various opposing factions on the one point on which all could agree — the need to oust the current administration—by coup, if necessary.

The Conservatives had been in power for over a decade, and government policies had tended generally to favor the rich landowners and keep the economy under foreign domination — a policy that had brought the worldwide economic depression of the 1930s to Argentina's doorstep. Widespread corruption, fraud, and use of force had also made many lose faith in the democratic process. As a result, there was a great reservoir of discontent in Argen-

UPI/BETTMANN NEWSPHOTOS

Ramón Castillo had been Conservative president during the "Infamous Decade," which was marked by government vote tampering. His overthrow was the result of emerging Argentine nationalism and resentment of foreign economic domination.

tina, and by 1943 support for the government had eroded. The time was right for a coup, if not a revolution. The president, Ramón Castillo, had handpicked as his successor a wealthy plantation owner, and the administration had every intention of indulging in electoral meddling — outright vote fraud — to ensure his election. In fact, the previous ten years of Conservative rule were known as the "Infamous Decade" because of the government's frequent use of vote tampering. Unfortunately, there was a great deal of precedent for this sort of illegality in Argentine history. The political opposition — remnants of the Radical party — immediately cast about for support among the military and initiated discussions with the minister of war, General Pedro Ramírez. When Castillo learned of it, he fired Ramírez and thereby precipitated a crisis. The officers of the GOU decided to act.

The Plaza de Mayo during the Revolution of 1943. Although Colonel Perón was a leading GOU member, he did not take part in the GOU coup; his inadequate explanations about his absence brought a reputation for cowardice.

AP/WIDE WORLD PHOTOS

And so, the Revolution of 1943 occurred on June 4, when General Arturo Rawson marched a phalanx of soldiers from the Campo de Mayo to the Casa Rosada. No army units in the city would come to the government's defense. Having no choice, Castillo resigned from office. Rawson assumed the presidency and appointed a cabinet. It all happened so quickly that many Argentines were left wondering what exactly had happened and why. Indeed, from the perspective of history, we do not have a much better view. The GOU was conservative — and so was Castillo's government. The GOU frowned on the concept of democracy — but the Conservatives were anything but democratic; in fact, they had elevated electoral fraud to a fine art. The GOU favored the Axis — and it so happened the Castillo government had recently come under fire from the United States for refusing to break off relations with Germany and Italy. There is one clue that makes the situation a little clearer. The conservative landowners of Argentina had longstanding economic and cultural ties with Britain — the British had been buying Argentine beef for the last hundred years. Therefore, the *estancieros*, the ranchers, were strongly pro-Allied.

Troops guarding the Casa Rosada during the Revolution of 1943. No army units in the city came to the Conservative government's defense; much of the military was either pro-Axis or neutral.

39

General Edelmiro Farrell replaced Ramírez as president after diplomatic relations with Axis countries were broken in 1944. Farrell was merely a figurehead leader; Perón exercised the real governmental power.

Much of the army was either pro-Axis or neutral. The Revolution of 1943 was essentially the result of the emergence of Argentine nationalism, coupled with the resentment of foreign economic domination. Many of Argentina's major companies were owned by the British, and this state of affairs was viewed by many Argentines as imperialism. The GOU was the focus of this sort of nationalist thinking, and taking advantage of the disrepute into which democracy had fallen during the fraud-tainted Infamous Decade, the GOU was able to succeed.

Perón vanished the day before the coup, did not participate in the march itself on June 4, and did not show up again until the day after, facts that led to later accusations of cowardice. He maintained that on June 4 he had been quelling a battle that had broken out by mistake between the marchers and sailors at a naval mechanics' school. This may be true, but Perón never gave an adequate account of what he did in those crucial hours.

At any rate, Argentina had a new government — which changed again two days later when Rawson lost favor with the GOU and was replaced with the former war minister, General Ramírez. Ramírez himself lasted less than a year, and the issue that caused his ouster was the persistent one of Argentina's diplomatic ties with the Axis. Ramírez finally gave into pressure from the United States and severed relations with Germany, Italy, and Japan early in 1944. The GOU disapproved, Ramírez was out, and General Edelmiro Farrell, who had been first the war minister, then vice-president, was in. Farrell, a weak leader, was little more than a figurehead.

According to U.S. intelligence reports of the time, the man orchestrating all the behind-the-scenes action was none other than Colonel Juan Perón. It was true to an extent. Perón's leadership qualities and personal magnetism had steadily been winning him support among the officer corps, and he took steps over a long period to increase that support and neutralize any opposition. Ramírez had appointed him head of the National Labor Department late in 1943 (a bone tossed to him that later proved to be his ultimate weapon), and Perón easily persuaded Farrell to appoint him minister of war. He later manipulated events and votes to have himself elected vice-president in July 1944, an election in which only top army officers voted.

Thus, Perón eventually became a powerful politician, with only the compliant Farrell his nominal superior. Perón still had enemies and would acquire more as time went on, including the United States, which was afraid of having a Fascist nation in the Western Hemisphere.

Perón's career was doing fine. His personal life, however, was rather empty. That was about to change.

Evita was about to appear on stage.

UPI/BETTMANN NEWSPHOTOS

Perón taking oath of office as minister of war in 1944. His leadership traits and personal magnetism won support from his fellow officers, and he used the influence of key government positions to gain an enormous popular following.

4

Evita

Perón was the first politician to recognize the potential role of organized labor in the political life of Argentina. By the time he became the head of the National Labor Department in October 1943, Argentine labor unions had been rendered virtually powerless by continual factional disputes. Socialists, Communists, and ideology-peddlers from other parties had competed for the political consciousness of the working class. A national labor organization, similar to the American AFL-CIO, had been set up in 1930. It was called the General Labor Confederation (the Spanish acronym was CGT). Its record of bringing about changes in government policy was not good. It, too, was beset by discord, so much so that by 1943 it had split in two.

World War II brought increased industrialization to Argentina, but the lot of the average worker did not improve by much. Living costs were constantly on the rise, and wages were not keeping up. Thus, the iron was hot for Perón to strike with, and he began the task of shaping worker discontent into an instrument of political power.

I put myself at his side. Perhaps this drew his attention to me, and when he had time to listen to me I spoke up as best I could: 'If, as you say, the cause of the people is your cause, however great the sacrifice, I will never leave your side until I die.'
—EVA PERÓN
on her first meeting
with Juan Perón

As worker support for Perón grew, political and intellectual opponents protested against the colonel's domination of the government in the mid-1940s. It was the new-found strength of organized labor that ultimately determined the course of Argentina's future.

A 1944 earthquake left the city of San Juan in rubble and caused over 10,000 deaths. Perón's work with government and private relief efforts led him to meet actress Eva Duarte for the first time.

Perón asked labor leaders to meet with him and discuss the problems of their memberships. Surprised, some did. They were even more surprised when Perón intervened in a violent labor strike and mediated a satisfactory settlement for the workers in October 1943. Things were obviously changing.

Perón urged the president to convert the National Labor Department into an agency with broader powers. The new Secretariat of Labor and Social Welfare (more simply known as the Labor Secretariat), now independent of the Ministry of the Interior, was a government entity responsible for the promotion of "social justice," a term that can mean many things, but usually means the process by which the lower classes gain an increased share of the wealth. The Labor Secretariat recommended new legislation to President Farrell, who dutifully signed it into law. The new laws dealt with retirement pensions, protection of the rights of workers to organize and strike, minimum wage scales, and other welfare and labor issues.

The Labor Secretariat encouraged the formation of new unions for workers who were not yet organized. Through the intervention of the secretariat, workers in existing unions began to get more favorable settlements in labor disputes.

Throughout Argentina, wages rose and working conditions improved. Many factory employees got paid holidays for the first time in their lives. In the eyes of Argentine workers, Perón was some sort of apparition, a suddenly appearing saint bestowing favors out of the blue. Who was this man, they must have wondered, this great benefactor of labor? Perón played the role to the hilt. He never passed up an opportunity to remind workers and labor leaders that he and he alone was responsible for the way things were going. Of course, Perón was right in making the claim, but labor officials, if not the workers themselves, knew that he was not acting out of the goodness of his heart. He wanted something in return — strong political support. This they were willing to give.

Perón (center) and Farrell (left) in parade for Argentine Independence Day in 1944. Their military government drew harsh criticism as "a hotbed of Nazi-Fascists," but working and living conditions for the poor were improving steadily.

Perón's motives were not entirely self-serving. He was still a military man, and he thought in terms of the national security. Argentina needed more industry, and labor unrest was not conducive to expansion and economic growth. Argentina especially needed a domestic arms industry, so that it could free itself from dependence on foreign countries for military equipment. Economic security, national security, worker security — in Perón's mind these three things were closely linked.

On January 15, 1944, a devastating earthquake hit the city of San Juan, Argentina, causing thousands of deaths and extensive damage. Perón ordered the Labor Secretariat to set up a relief effort and personally called upon the nation to contribute medicine, clothing, food, money, shelter, and blood. The response was immediate and enormous. People in the entertainment industry were quick to help, and a gala benefit show was put on at a stadium in Buenos Aires. Among those attending was Eva Duarte, a stage and radio actress. Perón showed up, and after the performance he and Eva struck up a conversation. They were seen leaving the stadium together.

The attraction between them was instantaneous and powerful. It was not long before they were living together and making no effort to keep the fact secret. Their relationship would change the course of Argentine history.

The woman who had captured Perón's heart was born on May 9, 1919, in the village of Los Toldas, which lies on the pampa west of Buenos Aires. She was baptized María Eva Ibarguren, and was the illegitimate offspring of Juan Duarte and his mistress, Juana Ibarguren. Eva always preferred to use her father's surname, even though it did not appear on her birth certificate. She grew up in genteel poverty, helping her mother run a boardinghouse, and left for the big city at 15 to pursue a career as an actress. After a few years of struggle in Buenos Aires, during which she played bit parts on stage, she finally became a well-known actress in radio soap operas.

Eva Duarte, popularly known as Evita, was a well-known radio actress in the 1940s. Her charismatic personality and political devotion to Perón won them both a fanatic cult following.

Evita — as she liked to be called — and Perón became inseparable, and their relationship became a political alliance as well as a personal bond. She took an active part in the formulation of policy and even wrote radio plays about the Peronist "Revolution." If one were to believe Evita, Perón alone was responsible for the coup of 1943. This sort of propaganda irritated other military officers to no end.

Propaganda or not, Perón needed all the help he could get, because he and his government were in trouble.

In late 1945 almost everyone hated the military government, from the Communists to the Conservatives, from the Socialists to the Radicals. The vic-

Martial law was declared in Buenos Aires on September 19, 1945, when an antigovernment "March for Freedom and the Constitution" called for free elections. Thousands were arrested, and Perón's authority was severely threatened.

General Eduardo Avalos led a group of military officers calling for Perón's ouster on October 9, 1945. Perón surprised many by swiftly stepping down; his resignation speech, however, cunningly rallied the support of labor.

torious Allies, especially the United States, were deeply suspicious of the military regime. Argentina had finally declared war against the Axis, but, ludicrously, it had been in March 1945, a scant two months before the final collapse of Nazi Germany. There was talk of escaped war criminals being given safe haven in Argentina. The opposition referred to the government as "a hotbed of Nazi-Fascists," and there had been a number of protest demonstrations. Joining, and even at times leading, the opposition was the U.S. ambassador to Argentina, Spruille Braden. He openly criticized the government and called on it to root out its Nazi-Fascist factions. Though he never mentioned Perón by name, he made no secret of his wish for the overthrow of the government. Perón cannily cast Braden's opposition as foreign intervention and so made his cause a nationalist one.

Perón had become the most important man in the government and was therefore the target of most of the criticism. He also had enemies in the Campo de Mayo. Some military officers opposed him on political grounds, others did so out of pure envy. Almost everyone in the officer corps disapproved of Evita. Not only did they find the couple's open cohabitation unseemly, they disapproved of what they felt was Evita's meddling in affairs of state. She was nothing but an empty-headed actress, they thought — and here she was, making political noises on the radio, talking about revolution as if this were some sort of socialist uprising. They certainly did not like the sound of it.

On September 19, 1945, a crowd of more than 400,000 people, organized by military factions and opposition parties, marched in the streets of Buenos Aires to show their disapproval of the "Nazi-Fascists" in the government. This "March for Freedom and the Constitution" sent shudders of fear through the government. A state of martial law was declared and thousands of people were arrested, some at the direct order of Perón. There were more demonstrations in the next few weeks, resulting in clashes between demonstrators and police. One newspaper was shut down, and there were many more arrests.

Over the next month Perón's position became increasingly shaky, and the Nicolini affair brought him down completely. Perón had Oscar Nicolini, a friend of Evita's family, named as director of the national postal service. The appointment enraged the officer corps at Campo de Mayo. Not only did they want one of their group to have the position, but they had also recently complained to Perón about Nicolini's alleged involvement in corruption. Perón had assured them he would take action. He was now an embarrassment to the rest of the military government. Plots hatched in Campo de Mayo, and on October 9, 1945, General Eduardo Avalos led a contingent of anti-Perón officers in revolt.

Perón fought back as well as he could, but his enemies had him checkmated. Avalos demanded that President Farrell ask Perón to resign. Perón capitulated. That he did so was surprising to some extent. As minister of war, he could have resisted with military force. He had enough friends in the army to carry off a countercoup with some chance of success. But he gave no such orders. Perhaps he gave in partly out of fear. There had been rumors of assassination plots, and, in truth, some officers had planned to shoot him.

On October 10 he made a farewell speech from the balcony of the Labor Secretariat building; the speech was broadcast over radio. In it he asked organized labor for support in the crisis. Workers understood. Perón was calling in the debts they owed him.

President Farrell was worried about the assassination plots. If Perón was killed, the workers might riot. Avalos agreed, and they decided to arrest Perón and put him under "protective custody."

On October 12, 1945, Perón waved to his aides from the deck of a navy ship that was to take him into political oblivion. It would be a very short stay.

News of Perón's resignation and subsequent arrest in October 1945 was cause for celebration among students and other antifascist groups in Buenos Aires.

UPI/BETTMANN NEWSPHOTOS

Mounted policemen move
through crowds demonstrat-
ing for Perón's release. The
government was reluctant to
test the true loyalties of police and army officers and allowed the demonstrations to
proceed.

Perón's "prison" was a small island off the coast.
He was confined to a comfortable cottage and allowed every amenity except his freedom. He wrote a
number of letters — to Evita, to his aides — and one
to General Avalos demanding his immediate release.
Avalos did not reply. Perón spent a lonely weekend.

Buenos Aires buzzed with rumors. The government was keeping Perón's whereabouts a secret.

Perón had courted the labor unions and had won
their enthusiastic support. When word got around
that he was in political trouble, that he might even
be in physical danger, union leaders quickly spread
the news to the membership. Strikes were called,
factories were shut down, and workers took to the
streets. There were some preliminary demonstrations, but they were broken up by the police. The
government viewed the situation with increasing
alarm. It was apparent that they had underestimated Perón's popularity.

On Tuesday, October 16, friends and supporters bargained successfully for Perón's release. Also, Perón complained of chest pains as a ruse for gaining his release. The government had agreed to his leaving the island to be admitted to the hospital for observation. So on Wednesday, October 17, 1945, Perón was back in Buenos Aires.

The government's grip on the situation was proving increasingly slippery. Not all of the army was behind General Avalos. Perón had backing among some of the younger officers. He knew that he could count on them, but he also knew that the government's hand had really been forced by the workers who were arriving in Buenos Aires by the truckload. Hordes of factory workers, meatpackers, and other laborers — derisively called *cabecitas negras*, or "little black heads" — had answered the call. Instead of raising their voices for higher wages and better working conditions, which they had recently won as a result of Perón's policies, they now shouted questions at the nervous faces that appeared in the windows of the Casa Rosada. "Where is Perón?" they demanded. "Where is the colonel? What have you done with him?" They wanted answers.

Many among the crowds of workers who awaited Perón's return to the Casa Rosada were shirtless; the name *descamisados* was used thereafter for Perón's unsophisticated loyalists.

UPI/BETTMANN NEWSPHOTOS

Perón's shrewd and confident waiting out of the October crisis ended in triumph for him; his political demands were met and Avalos was dismissed. He declared the demonstration of worker support for him a "celebration of democracy."

Inside the Casa Rosada, the government was worried. General Avalos gazed out the windows at the milling throng of discontented workers below. Afraid of the inevitable violence and its equally inevitable repercussions, he would not give the order to disperse the crowd. Out in the city, the police seemed either unable or unwilling to do anything about the demonstrations. It was known that some policemen were Perón supporters. Avalos feared a test of their loyalty to the government. He had resisted suggestions to use army troops to deal with the demonstrators. He did not want to risk a fight between pro- and anti-Perón officers. Avalos could only hope that after the crowd was satisfied that Perón was alive and well, after they had actually seen him, they would go home. But Perón was refusing Avalos's phone calls. Perón would come to the Casa Rosada, but in his own good time.

This was a war of nerves, and the only battlefield was the streets. In Argentina it was sometimes the case that whoever controlled the streets controlled the government. On October 17 the government was losing the battle of the Plaza de Mayo. Had Avalos acted early and decisively, the crisis might have been averted. Had he been willing to take the risk, he could have ordered the army to seal off downtown Buenos Aires. But now the rising tide of worker unrest threatened to flood the Casa Rosada itself. Avalos felt trapped, and he had no taste for desperate measures or heroic stands. This total failure of nerve on the part of the government did more than anything else to facilitate Perón's quick comeback.

Avalos eyed the scene dolefully. The night was hot, and the plaza seethed with shouting, sweaty, barechested workers.

"*Los descamisados,*" Avalos sneered. "The shirtless ones."

Thereafter, Perón's supporters would be known by that derogatory term. In time they would adopt the nickname with pride.

Presently, Avalos turned and faced his fellow officers, shrugging his braided shoulders. There was nothing to do but wait.

Meanwhile, Perón remained in his hospital suite, relishing the approaching moment of his triumph. What he had learned in Italy and Germany about political spectacle would now stand him in good stead. The crowd in the plaza was as primed and ready as any that had stood and patiently waited for Mussolini or Hitler.

Finally, Avalos caved in. All his attempts to calm the crowd had failed, and he was at his wits' end. He asked to meet with Perón, and the colonel agreed.

Avalos was driven to the hospital, where he met in private with Perón. An agreement was reached, and Perón shortly afterward left the hospital to meet with Farrell at the presidential residence. Having little choice, President Farrell acceded to all of Perón's demands. General Avalos was no longer in power. Farrell would appoint a new cabinet, and everyone in it would be a Perón supporter. This concession alone was enough to pave the way for Perón's triumphant return to power.

Thus, Perón's great moment had arrived, and when he stepped out on the balcony of the Casa Rosada, the crowds cheered him as no Argentine leader had been cheered before.

The crowd was not preoccupied with ideologies, or doctrines, or propaganda, but wanted only Colonel Perón. . . . It felt an almost religious devotion to him.
—the London *Times,* describing the mood on Oct. 17, 1945

5

The First Presidency

Avalos and the anti-Peronists had underestimated the extent of the colonel's working-class support. Not only that, they had made a fatal mistake in not assuring labor leaders that the gains recently won would be preserved. After the Avalos coup, some employers made it known that they would no longer give paid holidays. Workers feared the worst. They wanted the colonel back.

The October 17 demonstration in the Plaza de Mayo was the focal point of a nationwide general strike. No labor organization of any size opposed it. Argentina was shut down for two days. It shocked everybody. The Avalos government gave up, and Perón was out of prison and back in power.

But Perón was not yet president of Argentina. He had to be elected. A coalition of parties came together to back the candidate without a party: the new Labor party, the Nationalist Liberation Alliance, the Junta Renovadora (composed of ex-Radicals who had defected to Perón), and a few other conservative and nationalist splinter groups. The party platform advocated the nationalization of railroads and utilities, anti–big-business legislation, public works projects, and a host of social welfare measures.

> *As a government of the people, we have brought the people themselves into the government.*
> —JUAN PERÓN

A coalition of parties backed Perón's sweep of the February 1946 elections. His presidency proved to be a dictatorship based on essentially military concepts.

UPI/BETTMANN NEWSPHOTOS

Perón (left) receiving the sash of office from retiring President Farrell. In theory Peronism aimed for a middle road between capitalism and communism.

The opposition was disorganized. The Radicals nominated a presidential candidate, and the Socialists agreed to back him. So did other smaller parties; however, the Conservatives did nothing but stand on the sidelines. The Communists were finally admitted to the anti-Peronist coalition after some grumbling from the few trade union groups that opposed Perón. (Perón had stepped on some labor leaders' toes by setting up rival unions that put existing ones out of business.)

The campaign was marked by heated rhetoric and violence, most of the latter coming from the Peronist side. Perón denounced the violence, but his followers were not quick to obey. The United States exerted all the diplomatic pressure it could in an effort to discredit the colonel and boost the anti-Peronist candidates. But Perón denounced this as imperialist intervention, making the opposition appear to be unpatriotic.

The election was held on February 24, 1946, and was surprisingly untainted by violence or voting fraud. Early returns were interpreted as a victory for the opposition. But it was only wishful thinking. When all the ballots were counted, Perón had won by the largest electoral vote in Argentina's history. Peronist candidates rode the colonel's coattails to victory all over the country. Both houses of the legislature were now to be controlled by soldiers in Perón's personal army.

The triumph was now complete. Juan Domingo Perón was the constitutionally elected president of Argentina, enjoying the broadest-based popular support of any elected leader in the history of that country since Bartolomé Mitre. Argentines congratulated themselves, fully expecting that this flowering of democracy in their country would begin a golden age of freedom and prosperity.

The vigorous opposition to Perón's regime among the middle and upper classes had no effect against the electoral might of poorer Argentines. Their numbers alone assured Perón of a constant majority.

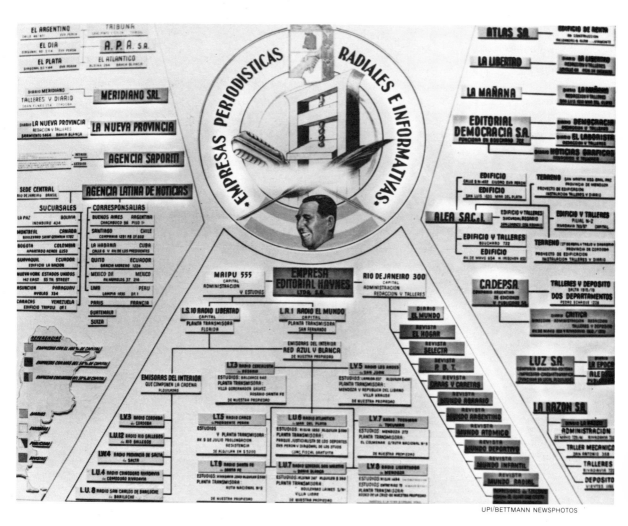

UPI/BETTMANN NEWSPHOTOS

This chart shows Perón as outright or partial owner of the major Argentine newspapers and radio stations. Public information and other social agencies were under his direct control.

Unfortunately, it was not to be.

Perón was the leader, Peronism was the movement. Even the name of the new, unified party formed from the coalition that backed his candidacy was changed to the Peronist party. In the Argentina of the late 1940s and early 1950s, the name Perón seemed to be everywhere and on everything.

Perón called his revolutionary political philosophy *justicialismo*. An equivalent term in English does not exist, but it could be rendered as "justicialism," a melding of the words "justice" and "socialism."

Perón saw his way of doing things as a middle road — or, as he put it, a "Third Position" — between the two opposing philosophies that divided the world: communism and capitalism. He held that the only just society is one in which various groups and social classes work together in an atmosphere of mutual trust and dedication to the common good. The key to this was unity, which meant, of course, unity under Perón and Peronism. The concept was based on military thinking. An army must be unified and well disciplined in order to be effective. If each soldier did as he pleased, no battles would be won. Orders are given, orders must be followed. This essentially military concept formed the core of Perón's thinking.

Unfortunately, translated into laws, directives, and policies, this philosophy tends to be antidemocratic. What is good for soldiers and armies is not necessarily good for countries or their citizens.

Perón casts his ballot in the 1948 national elections. The new constitution that was ratified shortly after the elections redefined political and economic rights in Peronist terms; democratic process was stripped to the bone, and governmental powers grew.

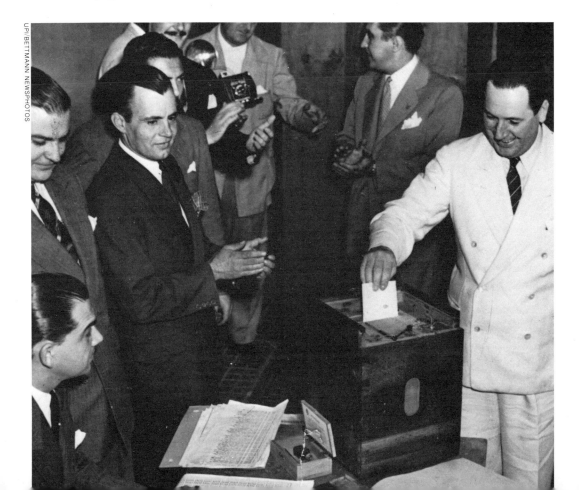

To achieve his concept of unity, Perón found it necessary to stifle dissent. In a series of crackdowns and government buyouts, the Peronist machine achieved almost total control of the media — the press, radio, and television. Political parties were denied the right of assembly and speech. Opposition legislators were censured and expelled, and eventually, many dissenters were jailed. Time for debate over legislation was cut short. It became a crime even to speak against the government — it was dangerous to criticize an official because it might be viewed as "disrespect," which was against the law.

There was to be no straying from the party line within the Peronist labor unions. Rumors circulated that the government had been behind an assassination attempt against Cipriano Reyes in July 1947. Reyes was a labor leader who had refused to abandon the original ideas of the Labor party. Even though the assassination had failed, the message was clear. Dissent from Peronism was, to say the least, not appreciated.

Evita Perón was her husband's most outspoken and effective propagandist, declaring to the Peronists, "He is God for us." Her strong personality and dramatic flair carried well via the state-controlled media.

UPI/BETTMAN NEWSPHOTOS

During her tour of Europe
Evita posed with this baby in
a Roman welfare hospital.
Her commitment to charitable causes in Argentina won
the adoration of the descamisados but depleted the
government treasury.

63

The Supreme Court of Argentina presented a problem to the Peronists. Three out of the five justices were hostile to the regime. Even though the grounds for prosecution were legal mumbo jumbo, the legislature tried and impeached each of the three justices. Perón appointed three new, Peronist justices. This effectively cleared the way for new Peronist legislation. There was hardly a chance of a government-backed law being declared unconstitutional with five solidly pro-Perón judges sitting on the bench.

A constitutional convention was called, and Peronist delegates began to rewrite Argentina's primary political document. Very important to Perón was Article 77, which forbade a president and vice-president from being elected to successive terms (meaning they could be elected a second time only after waiting out an intervening term). The article

Perón being driven to his second inauguration. He won reelection easily in November 1951 despite serious stress in the Argentine economy; a failed coup attempt indicated discontent among high-ranking officers.

was eliminated. The system of electors, copied from the U.S. electoral college, was also done away with. Presidential elections would henceforth be decided by popular vote. The new draft of the constitution became a Peronist document. It defined not just political rights but economic rights. Some were surprising concepts, such as "the right to acquire skill" and "the right to well-being." One might ask how any government could guarantee these things, especially the former, since a human being can acquire skill only if he possesses both talent and the will to succeed. A government can promote "well-being" by not harassing its citizens, but it can hardly guarantee happiness. The new document also defined workers' rights but was surprisingly silent on the right to strike. The truth was that there would be no strikes unless they were authorized by the government. This hardly put the worker in a position of strength. The new constitution contained other vague language that could be construed as legalizing the suppression of speech and political dissent. The opposition delegates vehemently objected, but they did not stop the new constitution from being adopted on March 11, 1949.

Even though the Perón delegates were generally well dressed, it could be said that the "shirtless ones" had successfully completed their takeover of the government.

Despite it all, however, not every Argentine citizen bowed his head at the mention of the general (Perón was promoted in 1949 by a special act of the legislature). The Peronist electoral majority was simply that, a majority, mainly made up of lower-class and lower-middle-class voters. Peronist support was lightest in the upper and upper-middle classes. Opposition to Perón was vigorous and widespread and especially bitter among the oligarchy, those who supported rule by the wealthy.

But Perón maintained his power well into the 1950s. After all, he was a legitimate, democratically elected leader. The Peronist majority held together for almost a decade. In the end Perón would yield only to an overwhelming force — his beloved comrades-in-arms.

We have made accessible to the people the road to culture and training. Thousands of working class sons are now free to decide their careers with the help of the instruction and training offered freely by the republic to her sons.
—JUAN PERÓN

Juan Perón and Eva Duarte were married on October 21, 1945. That put an end to the scandal of their living together, but the controversy surrounding their political partnership continues to this day.

Evita was busy. She campaigned passionately for women's suffrage, though she advocated a "feminism" that bears only faint resemblance to what is meant by the term today. A Peronist feminist, after Evita's example, accepted women's traditional responsibilities and directed her activism toward the cause of a man. Evita's cause was Juan Perón's; she was a tireless Peronist, propagandizing through every available medium, including a daily newspaper column (she owned the newspaper).

Evita, speaking about her husband said: "He is God for us . . . we cannot conceive of heaven without Perón. He is our sun, our air, our water, our life."

In 1947 she traveled to Europe. As a piece of stagecraft, if not foreign policy, it was a smash success. She was greeted by admiring crowds in Spain and was received as visiting royalty by the regime of the Spanish dictator Francisco Franco. She had an audience with the pope and was warmly welcomed by the French president, Vincent Auriol. Returning home in triumph, she moved her office into the building housing the Labor Secretariat. She now controlled the secretariat in all but name. Through an institution called the Eva Perón Foundation she controlled most of the charitable and welfare activity in the country, dispensing food, money, and medicine to needy people. The foundation also undertook the construction of much low-cost housing, children's hospitals, schools, homes for the elderly, and other worthy projects. She also ran the labor unions through the reunified, Peronist CGT (the Argentine equivalent of the AFL-CIO).

Evita was adored by the descamisados, and she developed a cult following. Her constant concern for the poor, the homeless, the old, and the sick made the masses look upon her as a saint. However, not everyone took this view. Evita was a controversial figure, and she drew as much criticism as she did adoration. The upper classes tended to view her as a scheming opportunist who had cynically manipulated people to get to the top. Some Argentines hated her, and some revile her even to this day. There is no doubt that she fully endorsed the Peronist mechanisms of oppression. She demanded and got the resignations of labor leaders and government officials who displeased her or threatened her total control of the Labor Secretariat. She was not above giving jobs to relatives and friends. Her brother Juan was made a private secretary to Perón. Friends received favors, enemies were given no quarter. To Evita, power was a means to achieve her goals. She had no doubt about the righteousness of her cause.

She was no saint. She was simply Evita.

By 1950 the economy of Argentina began to show signs of stress. Inflation was on the rise, and the nation's balance of international trade was unfavorable. Peronist policies were part of the cause. Social welfare programs had depleted the government treasury. High wages, though good for workers, discouraged the foreign investment that was also part of Perón's plan for increased industrialization. Perón's grip on labor was also loosening. Strikes in defiance of government policy broke out with increasing frequency.

In 1951 Evita's health failed. The year before she had been diagnosed as having cancer of the uterus, but she had rejected the doctor's advice and refused

On July 26, 1952, Evita Perón died. Cancer had been diagnosed two years earlier, but she refused the surgical treatment that might have saved her life.

to undergo a hysterectomy. She may have done so out of fear, maybe because of a deep distrust of the medical profession.

Rumors of anti-Perón plots circulated through the Campo de Mayo. An actual coup, led by a General Benjamin Menéndez, failed miserably in August 1951, but it was an indication of growing discontent among high-ranking officers. Perón blamed foreign meddling, darkly hinting that the United States was behind it all. His grip on the lever of power was still secure, however. He easily won reelection in November.

UPI/BETTMANN NEWSPHOTOS

The day of Evita's funeral was observed nationwide. Tens of thousands waited in rain-soaked lines to view her body; the outpouring of emotion surprised even Perón.

Evita's health deteriorated, and she finally underwent surgery. But it was too late. She died on July 26, 1952, and Argentina grieved. The country came to a halt on the day of her funeral. Tens of thousands of people filled the rain-soaked streets of Buenos Aires, waiting in line to view the body that lay in state at the Labor Secretariat, wanting to pay their last respects to "Saint Evita."

The outpouring of emotion surprised even Perón. "I did not know they loved her that much," he said.

He also did not know that it was the beginning of the end.

6

Second Presidency and Exile

The policies enacted during the first years of the Perón regime set the stage for the tragedy that followed.

By 1952 higher wages and government spending had led to a higher standard of living for workers but also had worsened inflation. Perón announced a cut in public expenditures and a two-year freeze on prices and wages. He also introduced austerity measures, such as meatless days and the substitution of black bread for white bread in the markets, instructing the populace to "consume less and produce more." An increasing amount of beef was being consumed in Argentina, leaving less for export. Perón countered by introducing agricultural subsidies and other measures to increase production of beef and wheat.

There were other problems. Allegations flew that corruption in the government was widespread. Acute shortages of meat in 1953 linked Evita's brother, Juan Duarte, to a bribery scheme. He committed suicide rather than face the investigation.

The attempt to systematize justicialismo *as a doctrine foundered upon the shoals created by Perón's flexibility fetish. He insisted not only upon cultivating vagueness but also glorifying it as a virtue.*
—JOSEPH A. PAGE
Perón biographer

Perón during a 1955 speech. Behind his outward confidence, Perón knew economic troubles and unfulfilled promises were eroding the groundwork of his second term. His own nerve would fail him at the end.

Peronism called for economic independence, which required full exploitation of domestic energy supplies. But Argentina was ill equipped for extensive oil and gas exploration, lacking both development funds and expertise. This meant the country needed to attract investment by foreign energy companies — which was embarrassing in light of Perón's constant haranguing against "imperialism from the north," by which, of course, he meant the United States. Nevertheless, in 1953 Perón began to court businessmen from North America, offering contract concessions that he had previously ruled out as imperialistic. In the spring of 1955, Standard Oil of California almost completed a deal that would have given it drilling rights in Patagonia for 40 years. But Perón's hold over the country was weakening, and the legislature refused to ratify the bill approving the contract. Even though Perón could justify the oil deal on many grounds, he lost face when it was defeated.

Beef hanging in storage. Perón's effort to turn the weak economy around included austerity measures in the early 1950s. Meatless days were introduced to increase the amounts of beef available for export.

UPI/BETTMANN NEWSPHOTOS

Juan Duarte, Evita's brother
and private secretary to Perón, committed suicide
rather than face corruption
charges linking him to acute
meat shortages in 1953. Perón's government was rid-
dled with corrupt officials.

Despite his mistakes he was still a demigod, if not
God Himself, in the eyes of the descamisados.
School children were taught to venerate him, statues of the general and Evita were everywhere, and
the name of Perón — it sometimes seemed — was on
every square and park and stadium in the country.

But much of the sense of mission had gone out
of the movement. Evita had been the beacon light
that guided Juan Perón's consolidation of absolute
power. With her death the light had failed. Throughout the country a sort of decay had set in. This is
usually the case with dictatorships. Creativity and
innovation are frowned upon, and when these qualities disappear a society tends to stagnate.

Perón's own dreams were fading. His goal had been to unite the country under his personal, dynamic leadership. He was a strong leader — in his mind, he was *born* for the role. This philosophy of leadership grew out of the Latin American concept of the caudillo, or strongman. As noted before, the provincial caudillos had played an active role in Argentina's early history. Their self-made empires were oftentimes oppressive and violent, but the caudillos held sway in the vacuum created by a weak central government. Perón was one of the last cau-

dillos, but his power was not unlimited. He had not yet realized his vision of a united, Peronist Argentina.

He resolved to try again. Leaders had to be strong, and sometimes they had to be harsh. If he could not animate the country by having its citizens worship a life-giving figure, he would galvanize them with hatred for an enemy. But all of Perón's old enemies had been vanquished. He looked for a new one, and he found it in — of all things — the Roman Catholic church.

Campaign rally in 1954. Although the Peronist movement outwardly looked much the same, its inner life and enthusiasm withered after the death of Evita. The Argentine economy stagnated.

Anti-Catholic demonstrators march in Buenos Aires in June 1955. Churches were burned in an illogical response to an attempted navy revolt. Peronists were torn between their faith and their politics.

Argentina was Catholic; even its constitution specified that the president of the nation had to be a communicant of the Church of Rome. Why Perón chose to provoke one of the most powerful institutions in Latin America, one that governed the spiritual lives of Peronists and anti-Peronists alike, will forever remain a mystery. Some observers have

theorized that Perón, like any dictator, could not long tolerate the existence of another source of power in the country. Some have guessed that Perón maintained a deep-seated resentment of the Catholic church that finally came to the surface. Others see Perón's attack as simply another episode in a long history of Latin American anticlericalism.

For whatever reason, Perón began his offensive in November 1954. He first accused the political opposition of sniping at Peronism from the sanctuary of the church. He then directly criticized the church itself for meddling in affairs of state. He went further than mere criticism; the Peronist legislature passed laws eliminating some religious holy days celebrated as government holidays. He introduced legislation that legalized divorce, which was forbidden by the Catholic church. The top clerics in the Catholic hierarchy strongly objected. Two priests, Manuel Tato and Ramón Nova, were deported as subversives and sent to Rome. Pope Pius XII responded with a decree excommunicating all those responsible for ordering and carrying out the expulsion. Perón's followers were more seriously shaken by the church's condemnation than was the general, though years later he would petition the Vatican to reinstate him as a Catholic.

Perón advocated the rapid secularization of Argentine society, which meant a sharper separation of church and state. Further measures to limit the power of the church were put before the legislature.

The reaction was immediate. For the first time, protests against the regime rose from sources other than the traditional opposition. Anti-Peronist pamphlets appeared, and devout Argentines filled the Plaza de Mayo to show support for the church.

Suddenly, on June 16, 1955, the Argentine navy rose in a stunning revolt. Naval aircraft bombed the Casa Rosada and other government buildings, causing hundreds of casualties among innocent bystanders. The insurrection was a complete failure and was put down in less than a day. In the aftermath, angry descamisados took to the streets and rioted, burning more than a dozen churches. It is not clear why they held the church responsible for something the military had done, but Perón's battles with the clergy must have been fresh in their memory. The mind of a mob is rarely logical.

The revolt shook Perón. The Peronist newspapers stopped printing articles critical of the church, and various other conciliatory gestures were made. The opposition was allowed to use nationalized radio for

the first time in years. But it was to no avail. Perón's coalition was unraveling, and many Peronists were torn between their faith and their politics.

On August 31 there came a surprise. Newspapers reported that Perón had resigned from office. But the opposition was suspicious, and no one was surprised when the "resignation" turned out to be merely a ploy. As it had so many times in the past, the Plaza de Mayo filled with descamisados shouting Perón's name, again demanding that he return to power. Again Perón made an appearance on the balcony to give a speech. This one was not conciliatory, however. He made no appeals for unity or forgiveness. Instead, he declared war on all opponents of his regime, no matter who they were. It was an open appeal for civilian violence, and it shocked even some Peronists.

Perón delivering an anticlerical speech in 1954. His sudden offensive against the powerful Roman Catholic church met unprecedented resistance and divided the Peronists.

UPI/BETTMANN NEWSPHOTOS

Soldiers loyal to Perón fought hard against a coordinated army and navy insurrection on September 16, 1955. Perón failed to press the defense of his regime, however, and he was forced to resign.

On September 16, 1955, army revolts flared up in several Argentine cities, and a naval task force blockaded Buenos Aires. This insurrection was much better coordinated than the disastrous revolt of June 16. Loyalist troops fought hard against the rebels, but the Casa Rosada seemed incapable of pressing the attack.

Then, a Peronist general went on the radio and read a letter from the president. In the letter, Perón made vague suggestions that he would resign if the national interest called for it.

The warring military factions called a truce and negotiated a settlement. Perón was out of the picture. There would be a new provisional government, a return to the old constitution, and elections. Until then, at least, the oligarchy would be in control again.

Juan Perón had come to the end of his presidency. His capitulation represented a failure of nerve as complete as the one that had originally allowed him to take power. Once he had bluffed a government into giving in; now he refused to call the rebels' bluff. He could have mobilized his descamisados to smother the insurrection, but he did not. Why?

Perhaps it was out of true patriotism. A prolonged civil war might have wiped out the progress he had worked so hard to achieve. Or, pragmatist to the last, he may have calculated the odds against him and decided that he simply could not win. Perhaps the real answer is that the moral rot that afflicted the country had also eaten away at Perón himself. He may just have lost faith in himself and the movement he had created.

False reports of Perón's resignation once again drew throngs of supporters to the Plaza de Mayo. They listened to an appeal for war against all opponents of his regime.

Perón took refuge in the Paraguayan embassy on September 20, 1955. From there he was granted safe passage to a navy gunboat docked in the harbor of Buenos Aires. The boat was to take him to exile in Paraguay.

> *I'm not sorry I didn't start a civil war. Many would have died, and the country would have been destroyed.*
>
> —JUAN PERÓN

Perón was granted passage aboard this Paraguayan warship several days after his fall from power. Years of exile lay ahead.

Once again, Juan Domingo Perón embarked on a journey to political oblivion. And again he would eventually return, but this time his exile would last a good deal longer. Perón would stay away from his homeland for almost two decades.

7

The Long Exile

Over the next five years, Juan Perón took refuge in several Latin American countries. Fleeing first to Paraguay, he then moved to Panama in November 1955. The next stop was Venezuela in August 1956, and after that the Dominican Republic in January 1958. In 1960 Perón left the New World to settle in Madrid, Spain, where he stayed for 13 years. He was not alone in his travels. Close aides and some old friends made up a small entourage. A new member joined the Perón family in Panama. Isabel Martínez, a nightclub dancer, was perhaps no replacement for Evita, but she quickly found a way to the general's heart. They were married in Spain.

During this time the situation in Argentina was anything but calm. The new government began a process of de-Peronization. Statues of the dictator were toppled, and his name was erased from everything that it had been engraved on. The Peronist party was outlawed, and many of its leaders were jailed. However, this did not mean that the Peronist movement was dead. On the contrary, a resistance movement came into being, its conspirators carrying on in the hope that one day their leader would return in triumph. Perón orchestrated the resistance from exile, communicating by hand-carried letters, tapes, and orally relayed instructions.

> *Though Juan Perón had committed and tolerated many excesses in his day, one thing that could be said for him was that he never converted his jails to slaughterhouses. The same could not be said for General Pedro E. Aramburu.*
> —JOSEPH A. PAGE
> Perón biographer, on
> Perón's political successor

Perón with foreign journalists in 1955. He insisted in interviews that he had never resigned the presidency. His influence on Argentine politics was to remain strong during his 17-year exile.

Buenos Aires students joined in the new government's effort to remove Perón's image and name from public places. Peronism reformed as a secret resistance movement.

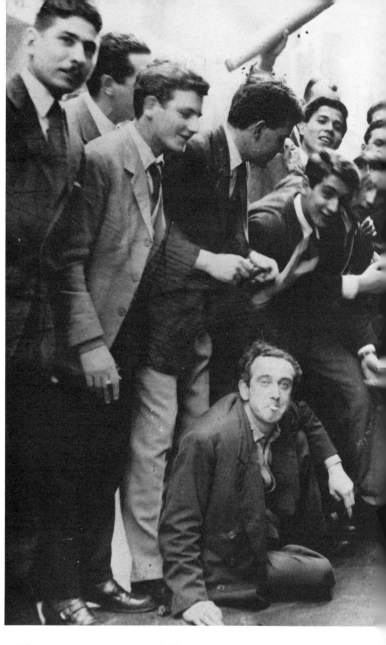

The movement was difficult to run. Until 1955 the various factions within the Peronist movement had been able to patch up their differences and march in step to the general's drum. But no more. There were now leftist Peronists — those who looked upon Peronism as a working-class cause — and orthodox Peronists, who wanted a wider social base. There were also neo-Peronists, who advocated "Peronism without Perón." They wanted the party to carry on the Perón tradition without his personal

leadership. Perón had to work with these factions in such a way as to prevent the movement from fragmenting and losing power.

Perón also tried to form coalitions with other political parties. After making a deal with Perón and receiving his endorsement, Arturo Frondizi, the candidate for the Intransigent Radical Civic Union, ran for president in the 1958 elections. (The Radical party had split into two groups — Frondizi's Intransigent Radicals and the People's Radical Civic

Isabel Martínez became the exiled Perón's new mistress and eventual wife. She carried his political messages to Argentina in the mid-1960s.

Union.) Frondizi drew millions of Peronist votes and won easily. But his economic programs turned out to be unfavorable to workers, and Perón eventually issued a denunciation of the new administration.

Perón moved to Spain because he had run out of Latin American countries that would take him. Spain and its right-wing dictator, Francisco Franco, saw in Perón an old pro-Axis ally. (Spain had been neutral in World War II, but during the war years Franco had maintained close ties to Germany, which had helped Franco's side in the Spanish civil war of the late 1930s.) But for all that, Perón was not exactly welcomed with enthusiasm. A controversial figure, he was a liability to any host government, and the Franco regime, though willing to help a friend in need, wanted as little trouble as possible.

Perón and Isabel settled down to life in exile. They were married on November 15, 1961, mostly for the sake of appearances and at the urging of their Spanish hosts. Perón also began to petition the Vatican to clear his name and reinstate him into the Catholic church. His reasons may have been more political than spiritual, given the Argentine constitution's requirement that the president be Roman Catholic.

Keeping a hand in Argentine politics was difficult at this distance, but Perón, ever the soldier, issued orders like a general behind the lines. Unfortunately, politics is not always as clear-cut as war strategy. Neo-Peronist parties had cropped up, and their leaders, although outwardly loyal to the general, did not always follow his directives to the letter. In March 1962 the Frondizi government fell when the military forced the president out of office. The generals and admirals allowed the president of the Senate, José María Guido, to take over as provisional chief executive instead of seizing power directly. As the real power behind the administration, the military could render Perón and Peronism powerless. The Peronist movement then splintered into more factions, creating further disunity.

Arturo Frondizi (center, left) won the presidency in 1958 with the help of Perón's endorsement. The military forced Frondizi out of office in 1962.

In 1963 Perón let it be known that he planned to return to Argentina but did not specify when. Peronists' hopes soared and rumors flew. On December 1, 1964, Perón left Spain without informing the Spanish government, or anyone else, by flying out on a regularly scheduled Iberia Airlines flight bound for Buenos Aires, with a stopover in Brazil. When the plane landed in Rio de Janeiro, Brazilian officials boarded it and demanded that Perón step off. He complied, protesting vehemently. It did him no good, because soon he and his companions were on the next flight back to Spain. The plane tickets for the flight out of Spain had been bought through a third party, and Perón had managed to slip through the heavy police guard around his house — but it was to no avail. Obviously, there had been a leak. It seemed that no one in the Western Hemisphere outside of Argentina wanted Perón to return.

General Juan Carlos Onganía took power by coup in 1966. His harsh dictatorial regime was destabilized in the late 1960s by leftist opponents.

General Roberto Levingston, an unknown to the public, became president of Argentina in June 1970. Radical movements with roots in Peronism used tactics of assassination and terrorism to counter his repressive policies.

Restrictions on Peronist parties eased in 1965, and Peronists of every stripe won seats in the legislature. Within the movement, the neo-Peronists gained strength. Perón sent Isabel back home to act as his emissary, and her presence in Argentina did much to boost the loyal Peronists, to the detriment of those who favored Peronism but not necessarily the general himself. Isabel made an especially big hit with the masses, the cabecitas negras, simply because she was Perón's woman. In her they saw a glimmer of the soul of Evita. Her mission was a success, but a sudden interruption of the political process made it an empty victory.

An army revolt overthrew the weak civilian government in June 1966. Led by General Juan Carlos Onganía, the coup was yet another attempt by top army brass to impose a harsh dictatorship on the people of Argentina in the name of law and order. The new government declared all political parties null and void and suspended the legislature. A long period of economic and political stagnation set in. The Peronist movement was driven underground, and when it surfaced again in 1968 it had a pronounced leftist coloration. Radical political views had become increasingly popular, especially among the young. The late 1960s heralded an era of student protests and civil disturbances all over the world. Argentina was no exception. In May 1969 a bloody revolt led by students and factory workers broke out in the city of Córdoba. Revolution was in the air.

Armed mounted police charge on demonstrators during violent clashes in the city of Córdoba in 1969. An attempted revolt by leftist students and factory workers failed, but it precipitated a shakeup in the Argentine leadership.

The revolt was put down, but it destabilized the Onganía regime and led to yet another military reshuffling of the top leadership. The new general in power was Roberto Levingston, army attaché at the Argentine embassy in Washington. A virtual unknown, he became president in June 1970.

A change at the top did not stop the radicalization of the Peronist movement or the increasing violence in the country. Various leftist underground organizations sprang up. Many of them had their roots in Peronism or found the goals of Peronism compatible with their own. Assassination and other acts of terrorism were part of their revolutionist plan of action. Perón himself did nothing to discourage these groups, and so gave them his tacit approval.

Demonstrators clash with police in the Andean city of Mendoza in 1972. Unchecked violence continued during the early 1970s despite repeated changes in leadership; acts of terrorism by extremists of the left and right multiplied.

Repression continued under Levingston, and so did civil upheavals. A second revolt in Córdoba made the generals lose faith in Levingston, and they replaced him with General Alejandro Lanusse, whom Perón had once jailed for taking part in an attempted coup. When he took the presidential oath of office in March 1971, Lanusse, like the original Radicals, was a believer in constitutional government and political freedom. He pledged free elections and the return of party politics, and he meant it. He hated Peronism, however, and hoped somehow to keep the party out of power without resorting to outright suppression.

President Alejandro Lanusse took office in March 1971. A believer in free elections and a longtime anti-Peronist, Lanusse nevertheless chose to drop a treason charge that had prevented Perón's return to Argentina.

Juan Perón in 1972. At 76 he saw his opportunity to return to Argentina. His tacit approval of the activities of leftist revolutionary groups helped manipulate his negotiations with Lanusse.

Perón recognized that his last chance for a return to power was at hand. He had grown old. He was approaching his 76th birthday, and the years were beginning to take their inevitable toll. It was now or never. He began to negotiate with the Lanusse administration, while at the same time applying pressure by keeping his Peronists stirred up. Lanusse gave in to several of Perón's demands. One was that several charges against the general, including treason, be dropped. This was the most crucial issue, and it paved the way, after further political bargaining, for Perón's eventual return to his homeland.

The long exile was over.

8

The Last Presidency

It was November 17, 1972. More than 17 years had passed since Juan Perón had left Argentina — 17 long, frustrating years. And now he was home.

His chartered plane was met at the airport by a select group of officials and journalists. The airport was under the strictest security, guarded by tanks and thousands of soldiers. Things went smoothly. The plane landed; Perón debarked and was driven away.

The Lanusse government was uneasy. Negotiations with Perón had broken down, and no one really knew Perón's intentions. Had he returned to run for office? To lead an insurrection? Or just to play elder statesman?

Perón remained cagey and noncommittal. Lanusse had issued a directive establishing a residency deadline of August 25 for all presidential candidates, requiring them to be in the country by that date. Perón had ignored the directive, calling it an attempt by the government to dictate the terms of his return. Perón had picked the date, and Perón had returned—but now what?

I carry in my ears what to me is the most remarkable music of all, the voice of the Argentine people.
—JUAN PERÓN

Perón's active return to Argentine politics rekindled faith in his vision of a unified society but did nothing to restore civil, economic, or political stability.

AP/WIDE WORLD PHOTOS

November 17, 1972: Perón arrives in Buenos Aires. Within a month he had formed a coalition to front a handpicked presidential candidate. In December he again left Argentina.

Perón needed a coalition. Better to confront the government with allies at one's side. Negotiations with the Radical factions had begun but eventually stalled. Other smaller political parties were more amenable, however, and in December 1972 a new party was born. It was called the Justicialist Liberation Front, the Spanish abbreviations spelling out FREJULI.

It was not Perón's intention to be the presidential candidate. Although he had scoffed at the residency requirement, he did not relish a clash with the government over this issue. Instead, he wanted another man to run — a man he could control. The man he chose was Héctor Cámpora, a loyal Peronist not noted for his outstanding leadership abilities. Everyone was surprised, and some descamisados were violently against Cámpora. But Perón prevailed. Cámpora received the nomination and was declared the FREJULI candidate.

His work done, Perón further shocked everybody by leaving Argentina to visit other countries and their leaders. He returned to Spain in December 1972.

The Peronists were back in power and won the presidential election of 1973. The campaign slogan was "Cámpora in office—Perón in power."

Héctor Cámpora, shown seated beneath a poster of Evita, was elected president in 1973 as a surrogate for Perón himself. The campaign slogan was, "Cámpora in office — Perón in power." The new president served ineptly for six months.

The office, however, proved too much for Cámpora's meager abilities. The left-wing Peronists were more numerous and more militant than ever before. Kidnapping and murder became alarmingly frequent. The universities were armed camps, run by leftist gangs. Most of these groups advocated a rapid move toward revolutionary socialism (also called Marxism-Leninism, after its founders). Strikes, sit-ins, and other demonstrations disrupted the nation on a daily basis. Cámpora did nothing to stop them. Argentina was on a downhill road to chaos.

Posters welcome Perón back to Argentina in June 1973. A million-strong crowd gathered at the airport, but shooting between rival Peronist factions provoked the worst civil violence in modern Argentine history.

Needing help, Cámpora went to Spain for consultation with the general in June 1973. Greatly displeased with Cámpora and with the situation back home, Perón announced that he was returning to Argentina.

This was it. This was to be the triumphal return to power that Perón had wanted for so many years. The first return had been a rehearsal, a little taste of what was to come. This time, the crowds would cheer, the bands would play, and it would be just like the Seventeenth of October again.

Crowds at Perón's third inauguration. In his final campaign Perón seemed committed to creating a distinctive Argentine populism that would straddle both sides of the political spectrum.

101

The event was planned as a day of glory for Perón and Peronism but ended as a day of the worst civil violence in modern Argentine history. On June 20 thousands of people waited at the airport, and perhaps a million lined the highway to Buenos Aires. Before Perón's airplane could touch down, a pitched battle broke out between leftist and orthodox, or loyalist, Peronists. Later, both sides gave conflicting reports as to who started the shooting and why, but when the firing stopped, hundreds of people lay dead on the grass. Perón's plane was diverted to another airport. His dream of a unified Argentina had again been dealt a setback.

To no one's surprise, Cámpora resigned on July 13, 1973. Some Peronists had been sure all along that the Cámpora presidency had been merely a ploy, a trick to pave the way for the general's final return. They may have been right, but there is reason to believe that Perón wanted Cámpora to serve a full term. Perón, in frail health, was approaching his 78th birthday. Shortly after the airport massacre, he suffered a mild heart attack. Although he recovered quickly, he must have known that he did not have long to live. Nevertheless, he went on nationwide television to say: "I will spend the last effort of my life to complete the mission that was entrusted to me."

The interim government announced new elections for September 23. There was no question as to who would be the next president. After much debate over the vice-presidential nomination, Perón requested that the Peronist convention delegates vote for his wife, Isabel. Ignoring loudly voiced protests, most of them complied.

Perón began the task of reconciling the warring Peronist factions — the young militants and the older trade-unionists. In a speech to a gathering of youth organizations on August 2, he drew the line at what he called "Marxist subversion," but stated that all other political philosophies were welcome in the movement. He expressed great confidence in Argentine youth, calling them the hope of the nation. The youth groups responded by issuing a statement in which they endorsed Perón's candidacy. Perón was so successful as a peacemaker that on August 31, leftists and orthodox Peronists marched side by side in a parade. They had been killing each other only two months before.

This was the Perón of old, the great unifier. He had always had a vision of leading a monolithic, 100 percent Peronist Argentina to glory, and now was his chance. In another speech he stressed the need for national reconciliation, appealing to other "political forces" in the country to put aside differences and join with him in a spirit of service to Argentina.

Young leftists marching in 1974. Perón betrayed leftist groups immediately after his election. Orders to purge radical elements from Peronist organizations led to endless arrests, assassinations, and counterviolence.

The elections went smoothly, with no violence or evidence of fraud. Perón won by a landslide. The Radical factions immediately assured Perón of their willingness to cooperate with the new administration. Even the military extended a conciliatory hand, and Perón's dream seemed on the verge of becoming reality. But it was not to be.

First came the crackdown on the leftists. Perón had used these groups in the past to destabilize the government, but now that he was in power, they were a liability. Directives were issued to all Peronist organizations, instructing them to purge themselves of "terrorists and subversive elements." A rash of assassinations followed; most of the victims were left-wing Peronists. These actions, however, only succeeded in driving the more extreme groups underground. In the aftermath, Peronist unity lay in shambles.

Violence continued as leftists retaliated. Four

Perón's funeral cortege proceeds through a Buenos Aires street on July 3, 1974. Argentina found some unity in mourning the controversial dictator's death. To his credit, Perón had given the working class an enduring self-awareness and cohesiveness.

UPI/BETTMANN NEWSPHOTOS

union leaders were assassinated during the three weeks following the general's election. In November a Ford Motor Company official was gunned down in the streets of Buenos Aires. When they weren't murdering people, extremist groups were kidnapping foreign business executives and holding them for ransom. With the money, they bought more guns and trained more assassins.

By May 1974 the nation was facing economic problems and an undoing of the unification that Perón's return to power had initially brought. Inflation, food shortages, unauthorized strikes, and general discontent rocked the Peronist ship of state.

Perón continued a full presidential schedule in spite of his failing health. In late June he came down with a viral lung infection, and his condition did not improve. On June 30, his heart showed the first signs of distress, and on Monday, July 1, 1974, Juan Perón suffered a cardiac arrest and died.

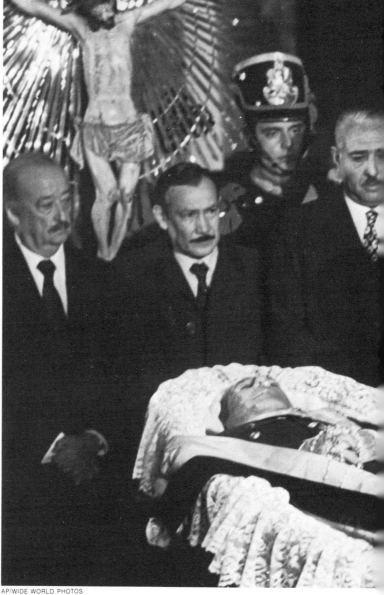

Juan Perón's widow, Isabel, views her husband's body lying in state; she briefly succeeded him as president. Peronism survived into the mid-1980s as an ideology that gradually evolved toward the European social-democratic model.

They all cried — the militant youth, the loyalists, the left, the right, and the center. They filed past his open coffin with tears streaming down their faces. It was like losing a father. It was as if a god had fallen from the heavens. Even his enemies felt a loss. For so long, Perón had been a massive, unavoidable feature of the political landscape, and it had been impossible to take a position without reference to him. One could be left of Perón or right of Perón. Now that the general was gone, there came a sense of losing one's bearings. There seemed to be no proper frame of reference.

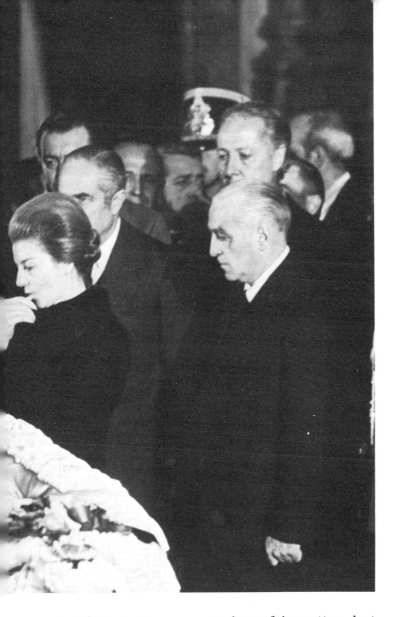

Isabel Perón became president of Argentina, but she did not last a year in office. The pendulum again swung the other way and the military ousted the civilian government on March 24, 1976. Democracy would return to Argentina only after a decade of the harshest, most repressive military rule the country had ever seen.

To this day, pictures of Perón and Evita are in the union halls and in the parlors of humble Argentine homes. Every now and then, someone sets a devotional candle to burn in front of them.

Saints? . . . or despots?

Further Reading

Alexander, Robert J. *Juan Domingo Perón: A History*. Boulder: Westview Press, 1979.

———. *The Perón Era*. New York: Columbia University Press, 1951.

Barnes, John. *Evita, First Lady*. New York: Grove Press, 1978.

Bourne, Richard. *Political Leaders in Latin America*. Baltimore: Penguin Books, 1969.

Fraser, Nicholas, and Marysa Navarro. *Eva Perón*. New York: W. W. Norton, 1980.

Page, Joseph A. *Perón: A Biography*. New York: Random House, 1983.

Smith, Peter H. *Argentina and the Failure of Democracy*. Madison: University of Wisconsin Press, 1974.

Turner, Frederick C., ed. *Juan Perón and the Reshaping of Argentina*. Pittsburgh: University of Pittsburgh Press, 1983.

Chronology

Oct. 8, 1895	Born Juan Domingo Perón in Lobos, Argentina
1911–13	Studies at the National Military Academy
Dec. 1913	Enters the infantry as a second lieutenant
Jan. 5, 1929	Marries Aurelia Tizón
1930–36	Teaches at war college and serves as aide in the war ministry
Sept. 6, 1930	Irigoyen regime overthrown by the military
1938	Aurelia Perón dies
1939–40	Perón lives in Italy to observe an Italian army division and serve as an attaché in the Argentine embassy
March 1942	Joins the pro-Axis Group of United Officers (GOU)
June 4, 1943	GOU overthrows the Castillo government
Oct. 1943	Perón appointed head of the National Labor Department
July 1944	Elected vice-president
Oct. 1945	Resigns the vice-presidency; taken into "protective custody" by the military
Oct. 17, 1945	Becomes Argentina's leader after massive displays of worker support
Oct. 21, 1945	Marries Eva Duarte in Buenos Aires
Feb. 24, 1946	Elected president
March 11, 1949	Peronist constitution adopted
Nov. 11, 1951	Perón is elected to a second presidential term
July 26, 1952	Evita Perón dies
June 16, 1955	Argentine navy stages an unsuccessful revolt
Sept. 1955	Perón forced out of office; flees to Paraguay
1960	Moves to Spain
Nov. 15, 1961	Marries Isabel Martínez
Dec. 1964	Attempts to return to Argentina but is turned back
Nov.–Dec. 1972	Visits Argentina; forms the Justicialist Liberation Front
June 20, 1973	Returns to Argentina amid civil strife
Sept. 23, 1973	Elected to a third term as president
July 1, 1974	Dies in Buenos Aires

Index

John DeChancie, the author of several published novels, is a free-lance writer who lives and works in western Pennsylvania.

Arthur M. Schlesinger, jr., taught history at Harvard for many years and is currently Albert Schweitzer Professor of the Humanities at City University of New York. He is the author of numerous highly praised works in American history and has twice been awarded the Pulitzer Prize. He served in the White House as special assistant to Presidents Kennedy and Johnson.

47701

47701

DATE	ISSUED TO
Spring '91	Jeanne M. Sikora

DATE DUE

Spring '91 FEB 0 2 2006			
APR 2 6 2006			

GAYLORD 334   PRINTED IN U. S. A.